A Trip To California In 1853

By

Washington Bailey

Edition : Culturea (culurea.fr), 34 Hérault
Contact : infos@culturea.fr
Impression : BOD, Norderstedt (Allemagne)
ISBN : 9791041983315
Date de publication : juillet 2023
Mise en page et maquettage : https://reedsy.com/
Cet ouvrage a été composé avec la police Bauer Bodoni

A Trip To California In 1853

CHAPTER I

UNCLE JOSHUA'S VISIT AND OUR PREPARATIONS FOR THE WEST

In the spring of 1853, my uncle, Joshua Bailey, came from California to Ohio to see his mother and his brothers, uncle John Bailey, and my father, Eben Bailey. But my father had moved to Fountain County, Indiana, so uncle Joshua came through Indiana to see us.

Joshua Bailey had gone to California in 1849, across the plains and had made over one hundred thousand dollars in gold. He hired my brother-in-law, William Reighley, to come out with him from Adams County, Ohio, to Indiana, to buy stock to take across the plains to California. My uncle had bought a span of mules in Ohio. Three of my cousins, William McNeal, Joel Bailey, George Bailey, and a man by the name of Bart Robins, brought the mules and some harness through to Indiana, so William Reighley, uncle Joshua and my cousins, were all together at my father's. My brother, Crawford Bailey, and my self, concluded to go along with them.

Uncle Joshua Bailey had gone to the lead mines when he was a young man, had married and raised his family there. It was from there he had gone to the gold mines. I was twenty-one year old at the time of uncle's visit to our house in Indiana, and it was the first time I had ever seen him.

My uncle poured out a pile of gold coins from a carpet sachel that was lined inside with buck skin and counted out several thousand dollars, enough to buy 250 head of cattle, 1,500 head of sheep and some horses and gave it to William Reighley, to go to Illinois to buy this stock and it did not look like you could hardly miss it out of the pile of gold coins on the table. He gave him more money than would be necessary to buy the stock and my brother, Crawford Bailey and cousin, William McNeal were to take what was left and pay the expense of feeding the stock and their lodging through to Indian Territory, where we were to start across the plains, and what was left, turn it over to uncle.

Wm. Reighley, for his labor buying the cattle and covering his expenses, kept out $50. He had traveled over 800 miles in coming to Illinois and traveling over Piatt, Macon, DeWitt, Logan, Tazwell and Peoria counties, picking up the stock. When the stock was finally delivered to uncle Joshua, he was well pleased with the judgment William used in the buying.

After uncle had made arrangements for the purchase of the stock, he went back to Wisconsin to his family and made preparations to move to California to make his home. After William Reighley had bought the stock in Illinois, he went with the boys as far as the Illinois River and then returned to Ohio. While the stock was being bought, I, with two other young men, were making preparations to go and overtake them. We had rented some land and had to dispose of that and sell some grain and some horses before starting.

We were to meet the advance party at Independence, Mo., but when we were ready to start, heavy rains had set in and we were much delayed by swollen streams. At many places we had to swim our horses as there were but few bridges. We had to go out of the way ten miles at Danville, in order to get across the Vermillion River. When we got to Peoria, we learned that the roads were so bad that we took passage on a steam boat down the Illinois River to St. Louis. There we took passage up the Missouri River to Independence, Mo., where we expected to find the men with the stock.

After reaching Independence and waiting several days, we were not able to hear anything of uncle or of the drove which he was driving through from Wisconsin. We learned that there were other places from which the overland trains started for the West. One was St. Joe, about eighty miles up the river, and two of my party went to St. Joe, while I remained at Independence. By watching at St. Joe and Independence, we expected to meet the train as we knew that we must be ahead of them. The men at St. Joe happened to run across uncle, who had been in St. Louis to buy supplies for the trip. They wrote me and I left for St. Joe.

We told uncle that he had instructed the men who were driving stock through from Illinois, to go to Independence, but he did not understand it that way. He had instructed his family and the men who were bringing the stock from Wisconsin, to go to Cainsville, Iowa, which was twenty-five miles above Council Bluffs on the Missouri River, and about 150 miles from St. Joe. Uncle bought a yoke of oxen and a wagon at St. Joe and he and I started for Cainsville.

After we were in Cainsville for several days, the family and party, with the horses, wagons and cattle, came from Wisconsin. In the party, were Peter Hughs, his brother-in-law and family, William Nailer, Thomas Roberts, John Teril, Allen Gilber, Horace Failling, Thomas Brooks, John Brooks and James Creek.

We remained there for two or three weeks, hoping to hear from the drove from Illinois. Uncle finally came to the conclusion that he had told them to go to Independence, Mo., and he sent Jobe Spray to St. Joe to see if he could find trace of them. He was given money to buy a horse and saddle, and in case they had crossed the river at St. Joe, he was to follow and overtake them, in order to get the two parties together. When he reached St. Joe, he found that they had crossed there and later learned that when crossing the Missouri, that they had stopped to shear the sheep, and on finding that Independence was south of the direct line, they had made directly for St. Joe and had crossed the river before Jobe had arrived. On account of the misunderstanding, uncle, with his party, was above Council Bluff on the east side of the Missouri, and the Illinois party was somewhere on the west side of the river in what is now Kansas.

I was with the party at Cainsville, when an incident happened which I never will forget. We were waiting for word from Jobe Spray, and uncle and all the party except one other man and myself had left the camp and gone to Cainsville. We were left to herd the cattle. While in the town, uncle met a man who owned a farm near the camp. They rode out as far as the camp together, and as uncle's horse was a little thin, having been ridden through from Wisconsin, and the farm was but a short distance away, he picketed out the horse, took off the saddle and threw it away far enough so that the horse could not reach it. He proceeded on foot to the man's farm.

From where I was herding, I could see the horse and went down, thinking that some of the party had come back from Cainsville, and that I would be able to get something to eat as I was very hungry. When I got to the camp, I saw that it was uncle's horse, but could not see anything of uncle. I started back to the cattle when I discovered the saddle in the grass with a two-bushel sack tied to the horn of the saddle. I was interested to know what was in the sack, thinking it might be crackers, so I gave the sack a kick with the toe of my boot. There was a jingling sound as if there were ox shoes and nails in it. So to satisfy my curiosity, I untied the sack from the saddle, ran my hand into it and took out, to my great surprise, a handful of gold. Tying up the sack, I looked in all directions for uncle, but could not see him. I called out for him as loud as I could, three or four time, but received no answer.

After waiting for quite awhile, I took the sack and hid it under some clothing and bedding in the bottom of one of the covered wagons. I then went to a high point near the cattle where I could watch both, the cattle and the wagon.

Along in the afternoon, the folks returned from Cainsville, and my mind was relieved, as I knew there was no further danger of prowlers. My helper and myself, gathered up the stock, and when we got into camp, it was dark and I was hungrier than I had ever been before in my life.

"Come to supper," was a welcome shout and the thought of the gold had vanished. While eating, I heard uncle call out to some of the men:

"Did you see anything of a sack on my saddle horn?"

Several of the men answered, "No," before I could get my mouth emptied and when my vocal canal was free from congestion, I holloed,

"I saw a sack on the horn of your saddle," and he answered back,

"All right Wash," and I told him to wait until I had my supper and I would be over and get it for him.

I went to the camp fire where the men were huddled and asked uncle where he had been and he said that he had walked to the farm across the fields. I asked him how much was in the sack and replied, "Thirty-six thousand Dollars."

I went to the wagon and got the sack. Uncle was badly scared and remarked that it was the most careless trick that he had ever done. There were some Mormons camped a short distance away and he said that if they had found the sack, that he would have been ruined.

While waiting at Cainsville, we finally received word from Jobe Spray that the Illinois party had crossed the river at St. Joe and had proceeded on west and that he would follow them, they having crossed the river two weeks before he got there. He had followed day and night and overtaken them about half way between St. Joe and Fort Kearney, which would be about 150 miles from St. Joe. After receiving the letter, we began to make arrangements to cross the Missouri River. The steam ferry boat had gone up the river after furs, so we had no way to get our stock and wagons across.

While waiting, a fur boat came down the river with three men. This boat was strictly a home made affair. It was built of rough sawed lumber and the bottom and sides were nailed onto the frame with several thicknesses of boards and caulked up with buffalo tallow to keep it from leaking too badly. We secured this boat to get us across.

The process of getting that old boat across the river was a difficult one and as it only could take sixteen cattle at a time, many trips had to be made. A round trip across the river, meant much labor, and was as follows:

After the cargo was put in the boat, it had to be hauled by ropes and pushed by pike poles up the river along the bank, until we were above an island which was in the middle of the river. Then we would cast off from the shore and by means of the oars, pulled for the opposite shore. The current, however, would take the boat in a diagonal direction so we would strike the lower end of the island. Then we would pull and push the old ark to the upper end of the island and again cast loose and finally reach the shore at a point much lower, being carried along with the current. In order to get back, we would drag the boat along the west shore to above the island again and cast off, reaching the lower end of the island. Dragging the boat along the shore to the upper end of the island and crossing, finally reach the east side below the camp. After two weeks of hard work, we managed to ferry all the stock and camp outfit across without serious accident.

CHAPTER II

ON THE WESTERN PLAINS – SOME OF OUR EXPERIENCES

When we reached the other side, we were in Indian territory, or what is now known as Nebraska, and a short distance north from where Omaha now is. At this place, uncle Joshua impressed on our minds the danger of an attack by the Indians and told us to make plenty of bullets and have our guns well loaded to protect ourselves. Up to this time, I had seen only two Indians. One of them was a squaw named Gripteth, on this side of the Wabash River in Warren County, Indiana. The other one I came upon lying in the grass south of Cainsville, wrapped up in a red blanket. The way uncle talked I thought that we would have to fight our way through. The imagination pictured out every bunch of grass or object in the distance as Indians, but coming closer, we found that we were always unnecessarily alarmed. The scare over meeting Indians gradually wore off, and when we came to the Indians, or rather, when they came to us, I was not as afraid of them as I was of the wolves.

We followed the Indian trail until we came to the Elkhorn River and there we crossed on a willow brush bridge. These bridges lay flat on the water and I did not find out how they were fastened to the banks. Before we reached California, we had crossed over several of them.

We kept a southwest course, following the trail and reached the Platte River, which we followed on the north side. We had traveled about 200 miles in Nebraska. We heard cannons firing and we knew that we were near Fort Kearney and that they were celebrating the Fourth of July.

Uncle Joshua, on a fine bay blooded mare which he had brought from Wisconsin, forded the river after a life and death struggle with the treacherous quick sands along the banks, and managed, by wading and swimming the horse, to get across the river.

After arriving on the opposite bank, he waved his hat in token of his success and started for the fort. He carried with him a seven shot Colts rifle and a five caliber Colts revolver. When uncle reached Fort Kearney, as we afterwards learned, he found that the Illinois train had passed through there two weeks before. Uncle took up the trail and after following for ten days, he overtook them on the south side of the North Platte, a short distance on this side of Fort Laramie near the Wyoming-Nebraska line, at a place called Ash Hollow. The river was forded and the cattle, sheep and horses were now on the right bank of the river.

The night after uncle had left the camp, we were camped near the river on some ground which was level and smooth. Aunt and her two children, Henry and Ellen, were with her in one of the tents. During the night there was a heavy rain or water spout. I was lying on the ground with my boots and coat under my head, and I was awakened by the water which had partly covered my body. I heard aunt crying and calling: "Where is Henry? I can't find Henry."

I started to go to her and got into deeper water and realized the water was raising very fast. I reached aunt, who was holding the little girl in her arms and she was hysterical about the boy. I heard a splash and following the direction of the sound in the darkness, I got my hand on his head and lifted him out of the water. I took aunt and the children to a covered wagon, where we stayed until morning. The water had raised until it was two and one-half feet deep, when it began to go down and by morning it was all gone. We were not able to understand where so much water came from so quickly or where it had gone, as the river was about a mile from the camp.

We broke camp and trailed on westward on the north side of the river, and after several days, we met uncle, who was returning from overtaking the Illinois train. He had halted them at Ash Hollow, near Fort Laramie. We finally reached their camp and for the first time after about a thousand miles' travel, the two trains were united.

It will be remembered that the junction place was to be Independence, Missouri, but the meeting place turned out to be in the borders of Wyoming. The two herds made 1500 sheep and 500 cattle and we were on the borders of the rough and tumble freaks of nature near the foot hills of the great Rockies.

After we had passed Fort Kearney in the month of July, we saw great herds of Buffalo going north. At times as we looked across the Platte River, we could see countless numbers of them and the earth would be black with them for miles. The droves would travel in "V" shape, with the leaders at the point. When a drove would cross the river toward us, it was necessary to use the utmost care in order that our cattle would not stampede. We would herd our cattle up close and get out with our guns and by shooting and holloing, we were able to turn the buffalo in a direction away from our cattle.

We came to high grounds, once, where there was excellent grazing and we stopped there for the day, to let the cattle and stock take advantage of the good grass. While we were eating our dinner, two Indians came riding up, with two of the finest spotted ponies I had ever seen. They got off and were holding them with a sort of a lariat, as they had no bridles, when Bart Robins, one of the men with us, made the Indians understand by signs, that he wanted to ride one of the ponies.

He mounted one of them and rode away to round some of the cattle which were straying. When Bart first started off, they did not care, but when they saw him circle away from the main herd, they evidently thought that he was running away with it, and one of them jumped on the other pony, fixed an arrow to his bow and started in pursuit. By yelling as loud as we could, we attracted the attention of Bart and motioned for him to circle back to camp. By keeping a circle, he kept out of shooting distance of the bow, and arrived in camp safe, but somewhat frightened over his experience. The Indians got on their ponies and left.

Two or three days after this incident, a chief and about twenty of his tribe, came to us and after a pow-wow, they sat down in a row and uncle understanding the maneuver, had as many of the men sit down facing them, as there were Indians. The chief lit his tomahock pipe, took a puff, passed it to uncle, who did the same. The order pursued, was that the chief would hand it to one of the Indians; the pipe would be returned to him, and he would hand it to uncle, who would give it to one of the men, who would return it to uncle, and uncle would give it back to the chief. The order was maintained until all the men and Indians had a puff at the pipe. When the program was over, the chief arose and said, "How!" and he and the Indians took their departure. This was the "pipe of peace" and meant that they would do us no harm, and we were not to harm them. Evidently this visit was to clear up the misunderstanding concerning the pony incident.

A rule had been made and understood by the men that there was to be no quarreling or fighting in the camp. It is unfortunate in camp life, especially on a trail far west, to have enmity in the camp. Tom Brooks, who was one of the cooks, was a crabbed fellow. James Greek was an orphan boy, who had made his home with uncle for several years, and who one day killed a big buffalo.

In order to preserve the meat, it was put through a process of jerking, which was to cut it into strips to be dried by the sun or by heating. We had made a scaffold by putting forked sticks in the ground and by laying sticks across in them, had made a platform about the fire. After the fire became a bed of charcoal, the meat was laid on the cross sticks to roast and dry.

James, who was a good natured chap of eighteen years of age, and having killed the buffalo, helped himself to a piece of the meat. Tom Brooks ordered him to put the meat back, which he refused to do, Tom jumping onto him and beat him, until his face was black with the beating. The sympathy of the camp was with Jim and Tom lost the respect of the camp by his bullying disposition. Uncle was restrained from taking a hand in the matter, as he could not afford to lose any of his helpers.

One day when uncle and aunt rode ahead to pick out a camping place, he had instructed us to drive the cattle to the left side of the trail as we were nearing alkali water, which was unfit for the stock to drink. He had given us wrong instructions, for instead of driving them away from the danger, we drove them to where they drank the injurious water. As a result, we lost, with what we had killed for beef, about 250 head of cattle. If the sheep drank any of the water, they were not affected.

In the herd of cattle we had left, were forty or fifty milk cows, some of them fresh and we had plenty of milk. The boys all milked except Wm. Nailor, who could not, but had made arrangements with the other boys to take his place and he would do some of their work in exchange.

One day, Nailor, who was in the rear of the train, came in late for dinner. It was customary for every one to have a cup of milk for dinner, and he held out his cup to Tom, the cook, for his milk. Tom, after the others had eaten, poured the milk out on the ground and said to Nailor, "No man who wont milk, can drink milk."

Nailor replied that he had made arrangement for others to milk in his place and that it was none of Tom's business. Angry words followed and Tom took a run at Nailor, butting him in the stomach. Nailor was knocked down, and in falling, his head struck the wheel of a wagon, cutting a gash in his scalp. This ended the fight and Tom, after this, was meaner than ever, as he had whipped Nailor, who had some reputation as a fighter.

It has been over sixty years since these events took place, but I distinctly remember another of the mean tricks of the cook. Tom had a way of cutting out of a side of bacon, the best part, leaving the balance for the family. My aunt spoke to him about it and with an oath, he told my aunt to attend to her own business. Such insolence was endured for the time being, but later Tom paid the penalty, the story of which will be told later.

I remember at one place where we camped late at night, that when we awoke the next morning, we discovered two graves side by side. Near the graves was an endgate of a wagon on which was cut with a knife, the words, "Do not camp here."

Evidently it was a dangerous place to camp on account of the Indians and the graves were mute testimony of that fact. The graves were lined with large rocks or bowlders, and over the top there were also rocks to protect the bodies from wolves. However, the wolves had dug down on one side deeper than the graves and dislodged some of the rocks and got the bodies. Some of the human bones were on the ground where the wolves left them after picking off the flesh.

We followed the headwaters of the North Platte, which flowed to the east, and leaving this river, we soon arrived at the headwaters of the Sweet River, whose waters flow westward into the Green River and on through the Columbia River to the Pacific. If you will take your atlas and find Fort Laramie on the Platte River, and follow it until you come to Casper, and then skirt the Rattlesnake hills on the north, you will reach the Sweet Water River near what is now called Independence Rock and Slit Rock.

The Sweet River Mountains will be on your south and the Wind Mountains on the north, as you cross between, through South Pass along the banks of the beautiful river Sweet Water. We saw the Chimney Rock which stood out by itself like a chimney after the house had burned. I think that it must be what is now called Independence Rock, which name is very appropriate. Also there was the Court House Rock, called that because of the rooms in it as if someone had cut rooms into the soft rock. There was the Devil's Gate, which was a massive ridge of rock, through which the river, some time in the dim past, had apparently drilled, and through the ages, disposed of the rock above, until a deep and straight-faced canyon greeted the "Path Finder" of other centuries.

We camped here for a day and others of the camp discovered a beautiful pool of water jutting out from the river. The water was clear as crystal and we could see in the water the most beautiful fish that I had ever seen. They were spotted or speckled and all about the same size—about twenty inches long. They were the speckled trout so much prized by the anglers of today.

We took one of uncle's wagon covers, tied a log chain to one side along the edge; tied a rope on the other side; got some tent poles and tied them to the end of the cover. We were going to seine this pool of water, when uncle came down to where we were and wanted to know what we were doing. We told him that we were going to seine the pool and catch some of those fine fish.

He said, "You can't catch fish with a wagon cover. You will only tear my cover to pieces and catch no fish. I don't want my cover torn up. I will need it."

We told him we would not hurt his wagon cover, but he forbade us using it. We told him that we had it fixed and we were going to make one haul any how, and show him we could catch fish with a wagon cover. Uncle got out of humor, but we did that once as we pleased. We went in with our seine at the upper end of the pool and dragged down to the lower end, where there was a nice gravel riffle, a nice place to pull out on the side. We boys had seined with uncle John's wagon cover in Elkrun in Ohio, and we understood the business. In the first haul, we had a lot of the finest kind of fish and uncle's wagon cover was not damaged.

Uncle was so surprised to see such a lot at one drag, that he told the men to unyoke the oxen, and that they could dress and fry fish the rest of the day. We caught all the fish they all wanted and as many as they wanted to take along.

CHAPTER III

AMONG THE FOOT HILLS AND TROUBLESOME INDIANS

If you will take your atlas, and look on the map of Wyoming, at the base of the Wind Mountains, the most rugged group of the Rockies, you will find South Pass, with the headwaters of the Sweetwater River, cutting a canyon through it. Going westward from this point and following the Sweetwater River, we came to the headwater, which was called Atlantic Springs. A few hundred yards beyond, we came to the Pacific Springs. This small strip of land is the water shed or dividing point between the two oceans. The water which bubbles up from the Atlantic Springs, races eastward through the rocky canyon of the Sweetwater and to the Platte and from the Platte to the Missouri, thence the Mississippi, uniting with the waters of the Ohio, Illinois, Tennesse and Cumberland, the Monongahela, of the Allegheny Mountains, finally reaching Gulf of Mexico and the Atlantic Ocean.

But should you follow the course of the sparkling water that gushes from the Pacific Springs, you would course along the Big Sandy to the Green River, which cuts its way through the sand and rocks of that rough and tumble country of northern Utah and northwestern Colorado. Launch your boat on the turbulent waters and drift, if you were not capsized, in southern Utah, you would come to Colorado River and then soon in the shadows of the most wonderful canyons which scar Mother Earth, the Cataract, Marble and Grand Canyons, of world renown. These livid seething waters find rest in the bosom of the great Pacific.

We trailed westward across the Pacific Springs toward the Bear River which flowed south to Bear Lake in the northern part of Utah. We were on what was called Fremont and Carson route. This lead southwest to Salt Lake City. When northeast of Salt Lake City, we came to what was called the Truckey route. This route left Salt Lake City to our left. We were behind all the other trains and it had been reported that the Mormons had killed a whole train of men, women and children, for plunder and had laid it onto the Indians. Old Brigham Young had sent what he called his "Destroying Angels" and had murdered all of them and took all the stock and wagons.

We decided to take the Truckey route and keep away from Brigham Young and his "destroying angels."

Perhaps one of the most interesting things I saw while traveling through the Bear River country in southern Utah, was a lava bed, about fifty or sixty feet high and I judge about two hundred feet wide at the base. At the crest, the lava was bubbling out as clear as water and running down the side of the mound, it would cool and turn into rock, forming a rocky mound. I saw three such mounds of lava or rock, which had been formed this way. The soil in the Bear River bottom was rich, black soil, and I thought what a pity it was that it should be covered with these mounds of lava.

There was a grave at the foot of this mound with a head board, on which we were informed that the deceased had drunk of the lava water and had died in a few minutes and that the water was poison.

We came across what was called Soda Springs and the water was as fine as any I had ever drank, and it came out of the ground foaming, a veritable natural soda water fountain. We also saw the Steam Boat Springs, which gushed from a hole in the basin of rock. The water was boiling hot and it bubbled and sizzled like boiling water on a stove. It would boil for a short time and then the steam would shoot up about fifteen feet high. Below this spring and near the river, was a strip of rocks about twenty feet wide, that seemed to be in motion with heat. The water in the river was so hot we could not hold our hands in it for two or three rods along the banks.

Down the river and off to one side, we came to Bear Rock. This rock was cut up with great crevices and if a man or beast had fallen into one of them, they would have disappeared from view in the bowels of the earth. I threw a rock into one of them and heard it rattling down into the depths until the sound gradually died away in what appeared to be bottomless. This serrated rock appeared to be about three miles across and it was the most dangerous place we had encountered. It had to be crossed as it was the path of the trail. A road had been made by wedging rock in the crevices and by means of picks, the way had been smoothed down so we were able to get across without serious accident.

While near Bear River, James Bailey and John Teril were driving a cow whose feet were so worn that she could not keep up with the rest of the drove. The boys would drive her along slowly and arrive late in the evening at the camp. She was a big red cow and uncle hated to lose her, but one evening she laid down and the boys could not whip her up and they had to come to camp without her. The next morning uncle sent Jim and I after her. As we came in sight of her, an awful sight came to our view. A pack of wolves were around her, snarling and gnashing on all sides. The cow was making a desperate struggle to keep off the ravenous wolves. When we saw the condition, we rode as fast as we could and the wolves took to the tall grass. We found the hind quarter of the cow bleeding and in some places the flesh was stripped off to the bone. There was nothing to do but to put her out of her misery, which I did with a shot from my gun.

Jim held my horse and I went near enough to the grass to shoot at them as they ventured out of the grass. I could not tell whether I killed any of them or not as they would leap back in the grass. I had in mind to go nearer to the grass to see the result of my shots, when Jim called to me and said, "Wash, come quick. Get on your horse, the grass is alive with them."

When I got on my horse, I could see on both sides of the trail the grass all in motion with the cat like movements of the wolves. We could not see them, but the waving grass showed that it was full of them. We put spurs to our horses and when we got to a safe distance, we stopped and looked back. The wolves had come out of the grass and were pilled upon the cow, resembling a small hay stack.

One day soon after this, when we had made a noon stop, an Indian chief, who could talk our language, told us that his men, while hunting, had found a white man who was nearly starved to death, and that he had carried him to his lodge. Uncle and some more of the men went with him to see if he was strong enough to be taken along. They found him too weak to be moved. After a council between uncle and the chief, it was decided to leave him there and the chief promised to look after him and when he was strong enough, that he would put him on a pony and send him to Salt Lake

City. I believe the man was left in good hands and that the chief was a man of his word.

We were now coming to the desert country of Nevada and our cattle had been without water for a day, when we came to what is known as Poison Water. To get across this little stream, we put the cattle in bunches of twelve and whipped them across, not letting them stop to drink. We got all of our stock across without being poisoned. After we got across, on the side of the hill, we saw the awful effects of the poison water, as there were hundreds of dead cattle and rods at a time, we could step on dead cattle without stepping on the ground.

After we got back on the Freemont and Carson route and were making for the headwaters of the Humbolt River, we found some fair grass land for the stock. We followed the Humbolt River for many miles until we came to the Humbolt Sink. At first it was as smooth as a rock for some distance, but later we dropped off into sand and it was the worst travelling I ever saw. The sand was so light and fine, that one foot would go down until I would set the other foot on top of the sand and pull that foot out, before I could step one foot ahead of the other. It was about the same sort of motion and as slow as treading water. We were three days and nights crossing that desert.

After getting across this desert stretch, we came to the banks of the Carson River, which we were to follow for many miles to the borders of California. When we reached Carson River, we came to a trader's pound, constructed of wagon tires and log chains. It was about the size of an ordinary city lot. There were tires lengthwise and crosswise, hind wheel tires, front wheel tires and log chains, bound together in all kinds of shapes. There were tons of steel in that fence. We came across another pound on the Carson River, near the Sierra Nevada Mountains, built of logs. The logs were 100 feet or over in length and had notches cut in them. These logs were placed in two rows and were crossed by small logs resting in the notches. It was built high enough so that stock could not jump over.

One night when we were afraid the Indians would come in on us, a double guard was put on duty. Four men stood guard in the fore part of the night and four in the after part. The eight men to do duty were all the men in my mess. Uncle said that the bacon was getting low and that he wanted some one of our mess, to get up early and help kill a beef. I told him to have some of the men in the other mess to help, as we would be on guard duty all night. Uncle said, "All right."

The men of my mess had killed all the beeves and mutton up to that time. We did not care, nor did we think much about it, as one of our men was a butcher. The next morning uncle called for some one to get up and help him kill a beef. He called the second and third time, and no one got up and he said, "If no one will get up and help, you will do without meat."

Two of the men in my mess said, "If the other fellows will not help, we will."

I did not help as I was willing to do without meat rather than help after being on guard about all night. When I got up, I went over to the other camp to see what was the matter and why they would not help to kill the beef. They had all gone to look after the stock except John and Tom Brooks. Tom, the cook, did not have to help with the other work. I asked, "John, why did not you fellows get up this morning and help uncle?"

He looked at me, wrinkled up his face, swore and said as hateful as he could, "You will be a good deal prettier than you are, before I will help kill a beef."

"Johnny," I replied, "If you don't propose to do your part, you might get a dose you would not like so well."

I thought I would go back to my camp and say nothing more about it. I started off and had gone about a rod, when John said, "Now you go off to your own camp, or I will put Tom at you."

I turned around and looked at him and remarked, "You low lived insignificant scoundrel, you will put Tom at me?"

"Yes, and if you don't go to your own home, I will get at you," Tom cut in.

"You big necked, nigerfied, curly-headed villian, you will get at me?" I replied.

At that he came running toward me and as he came near, he ducked his head to butt me in the stomach. When I saw that, I ran backwards a little to kill the shock and I reached down and caught him in the cheek, gave him a jerk, and he fell on his back. He fell near the hind wheel of a wagon. He pulled himself up by holding to the wheel and I got him by the throat and pushed him back between the wheel and the bed, and beat his face and head like he did poor Jim Greek and gave him some for Nailor and some for abusing aunt, and some for jumping on to me. When I got through, he had a plenty and the great fighter was badly whipped and he had not given me a scratch.

This was the first fight I had ever had and I found out afterwards that he had told the boys, that if any of his mess helped kill the beef, they would have had him to whip first. Aunt saw the commotion and called for me to come to their camp fire and get my breakfast. She said, "I am going to give you the best breakfast you ever had on the plains, for whipping that low lived, good for nothing, Tom Brooks."

I ate breakfast with aunt—was the best meal on the plains and the only time I had eaten with her. Tom Brooks behaved after that.

One morning we missed a cow out of the herd. Several of us went to find her. We hunted for quite a while and finally all came back to camp with the exception of my brother, Crawford Bailey and Wint Crumley. There was a willow thicket along the river and they got out of sight of us. They had found the trail of the cow and followed it. The camp had moved on down the trail while George Bailey had taken his gun and went on foot to kill an antelope. While hunting on the side of the trail, he was surprised to see Crawford and Wint running their horses around a bend in the river. He made for the trail just in time to catch one of the horses by the tail and by that means, kept up with the fleeing men. The Indians who were after them, tried to cut them off, but when they came in sight of the camp, they gave up the chase and disappeared. The two boys had followed the track of the cow into a willow thicket and they came across the Indians with a cow's hide stretched across poles, scrapping it ready for tanning. The Indians saw them and gave chase, but the fleetness of the horses and George's lucky hold on the tail of the horse, saved their scalps.

A few nights after this incident, we had to drive late to get to where there was a good place to camp. It was dusk when we camped. We had to turn off to the right of the main trail and the river bent off to the north and I think it was a quarter of a mile from the main trail to where we camped. We had built our fires and were just ready to commence getting supper, when we heard the Indians begin holloing, "Show shony, show shony, humbugen, humbugen oss cawaw cawaw, cawowaw cawowaw cawowaw cawaw cawaw."

The first time they holloed this, uncle Joshua Bailey said, "There! We are going to be attacked. That is the war whoop. Put out the fires and corral the wagons."

The wagons were placed in a circle, running the tongues under each other so we could get inside and protect ourselves from their arrows as much as possible. When we got that done, which was in short order, he said, "All hands load your guns and your revolvers and have your knives ready."

We had been so long on the road that everybody had become careless. Some of the guns had not been used for a long time and were rusty and others had no bullets. Some had to prepare their guns, while others tried to run bullets. We had what we called ladles to melt lead in. They were made of wooden pieces split out of oak or some other kind of hard timber, four square, with one end hewed round for the handle, the other end, that is, the square end, had a hole cut down in with the corner of the ax. We would put lead in this ladle and put coals of fire in on the lead and blow the coals with our breath, and which would not make much light.

Joel Bailey, my cousin, had run off from home when a small boy, got on a steam boat at Ripley, Ohio, worked his passage as dish washer, and had gone to Wisconsin, where my three uncles were. While there, Joel got acquainted with the Indians and their ways more than I did, but I had got pretty well acquainted by this time myself.

Aunt Susan Bailey was crying and talking to uncle and saying, "O, Bailey, why did you bring us all out here to be killed by the Indians."

"We had treaties and I did not think they would bother us," replied uncle.

Bellry Bailey, their eldest daughter, was of age, and Rachel Ann, the next daughter, was nearly of age, together with Aunt Susan and the rest of the little boys and girls of the camp were crying, and there in the utter darkness, it was hard to tell who were or were not crying.

Joel Bailey, I knew, was a coward when he was sober, but when under the influence of liquor, he was not afraid of anything. All at once he holloed out, "If any other man will go with me, we will go out and see what those fellows want."

I thought he was doing it for bluff, so I said, "I'll go with you."

"Well, go and equip yourself," answered Joel.

I replied, "What kind of equipment do you want me to have, a double barreled rifle, shotgun and a Colts revolver and a bowie-knife?"

We had some of the guns in order, having been used for hunting purposes and Joel and I knew it, but someone handed me a Colts revolver, for they knew I had only a single barreled pistol; another a combination gun, which had a rifle barrel and shot gun barrel on the same stock. Joel was equipped by the time I was. The Indians commenced holloing again, up the river behind us, where we had come just before camping. They would come down closer and then stop and hollo the same words. I will never forget them while I live.

We started out and the men began to beg us not to go, for they thought we would be killed. I informed them that I had promised to go and that I was going to go if Joel did not back out. The Indians by this time had located our camp and were holloing again. Uncle Joshua came outside the wagons, got one foot on the hub of the hind wheel, held to the bow of the wagon cover, and plead for us to come back and all fight and die together. Joel turned and told him with an oath, that if he didn't hush, he would shoot him, so uncle said no more. It was an awful dark night and one could not tell one another at all, only by bulk and that not more than a few feet from each other. We walked straight as we could toward the sound of the Indians' voices. We got out of the sound of the crying and lamenting at the camp and Joel said, "Wash, I want to tell you something. I have been drinking wine and my head is not exactly level and I will have to depend on you to do the guessing for me."

Later we heard voices and Joel whispered, "There are the chiefs giving the command and if we can get them, we can save the train, that is if we can get them before you hear the screech raise in the camp. But if you hear the screech raise in the camp before we get the chiefs, we will have to give leg bail for security, for we are all the ones that will get out alive."

"Where did you get your wine," I asked.

"In that wagon I am driving," said Joel. "Uncle Josh has a keg of wine in that wagon and if we can get those chiefs, you shall have wine to drink as long as that keg lasts."

I did not know there had been a bit of liquor of any kind in the train for over two thousand miles and I was puzzled to know what to do with a man under the influence of wine, whether to go back to camp or go on and try to take the chiefs. But I concluded to go ahead and try it, for Joel had said that the Indians would do nothing without their chiefs first giving the command.

The chiefs kept going on west and north, circling around our camp. Every time they would hollo, giving commands to their tribe, we would have to change our course and go more to our right in order to follow their voices, for that was all we had to go by, for a man could not see six feet to tell where they were. The chiefs got straight west of us down the river below our camp. I think fully a mile from our camp, and we could hear over a mile on a still night.

The chiefs stopped and remained in one place and holloed the same "Show shoney humbugen oss humbugen oss cawaw cawaw cawowaw cawowaw cawaw cawaw." I could tell by the sound of their voices, after I got pretty close to them, that they laid down every time they holloed. Joel had told me that when close enough and thought I could guess the distance, we must count our steps and walk right straight to the sound of their voices. When we had stepped to where I thought they were, for me to stop and he would hollo as loud as he could, "howdy doo."

"They can't keep their mouth shut and they will say 'howdy doo' too, then you show one of them how you do and I will show the other one how I do. Take him or die. Kill him if you have to take him dead, and I will take the other one or I'll die."

We stationed ourselves to where their voices sounded close to us, and when they holloed again, I whispered to Joel, "About fifty steps, Joel, for your life."

I don't believe I missed it two feet. Joel's head was level enough to count his steps right, for we both stopped at once. As we went along, Joel bore over toward me. I was taller than he. I kept holding him over to the left, for I thought he was trying to go too far to the right for the sound of their voices. When we got to where they were laying in the grass, they were several feet apart. We were between them.

"How do you do?" holloed Joel.

"Howdy doo," said the Indian at my right.

Joel jumped across in front of me, right onto the Indian, and said with a big word, "I'll show you how I do."

As Joel passed in front of me, I looked quickly over to my left, for the voice I had been listening to. It sounded more to the left, when I saw something in the dark. I thought it might be the other Indian's head. I jumped toward it. When I lit, I could see the object more plainly and I made the second jump as far as I could and grabbed with my left hand. My fingers struck his head under the plat of his hair. He pulled and twisted, thrust his feet forward and threw his weight on my arm, but I jammed him up by the hair and told him if he made a move to hurt me, I would cut his heart out.

"O, Wash!" called Joel, "Have you got your'n?"

"Yes," I replied, "I've got him by the hair of his head, with my left hand behind his back, and my bowie-knife drawn on him, and if he makes a move to hurt me, I'll cut his heart out. Have you got yours?"

"I've got him in the same fix," was the reply.

As we talked, we were pushing toward each other, until I could see Joel and his Indian. I told Joel not to get too close, so that if they go to do anything, we wouldn't hurt each other.

When we neared the camp, uncle Joshua holloed, "Boys, have you got 'em?"

"Yes, we've got 'em," said Joel.

Uncle evidently did not hear and he yelled, "O, Wash, have you got 'em?"

"Yes," I holloed as loud as I could, "I've got one by the hair of his head and I'll cut his heart out if he makes a bad move. Joel's got his in the same fix."

"Hold on to them boys," uncle said, "Hold on to them." I holloed back, "Start up the fires so we can see where to come," and the fires lit up mighty quick.

I shoved up on my Indian's hair and made him tramp up. When we got to where Aunt Susan Bailey, Bellry and Rachel could see us with the Indians, they commenced to jump up and down and clap their hands, exclaiming, "O, Goody, goody," the tears running down their faces. The little boys and girls all joined in.

When the camp got more settled, the other men started out to look after the stock and we had uncle with his seven shot Colt rifle watching the Indians. Joel and I untied the Indians' belts and took their tomahocks, knives, bows and arrows from them. Each had a fox skin full of arrows. We were going to hide them, when all at once the Indian I had taken in, commenced holloing, "Show shoney humbugen—"

But that was as far as he got, when we holloed to uncle, "Knock him down, knock him down, don't let him hollo."

We dropped the belts and Indian weapons and ran back with our fists shut, ready to strike as soon as we could get to him. Uncle had his fist dawn to strike, but grabbed his Colts rifle which was leaning against a wagon, and drew his gun on them both and said, "Drop to the ground or I'll blow both your brains out."

They dropped flat on their faces.

"Now," said uncle, "If you fellows move or say a word until tomorrow morning at sun up, I'll blow your brains out."

They lay there all night and did not move until after sun up the next morning.

The men gathered up the stock and saw to them as well as they could and then came in and got their suppers. It was getting late by this time. Uncle sat in his place and watched the Indians all night. All the men guarded the stock and the camp except Joel and I. The men told us that we were excused from further duty and that Joel and I might go to bed and sleep. We were the only men in the train that slept any that night. I don't believe the women slept much either.

The next morning we held a council concerning these chiefs. Uncle had more experience with Indians than the rest of us.

"If we kill them," said uncle, "The whole tribe might come on us, and if we took them along, the other Indians would see us and they might come onto us and overpower us. The best thing we can do, is to give them their breakfast and treat them well and let them go, and maybe they'll not bother us any more."

This we did. That morning we got a late start. The sun was way up and it must have been about nine o'clock before we drove out.

While we were eating our dinner the following day, some Indians came to us—one was a chief of another tribe. He was an educated chief and could talk our language. We had just gotten out of the tribe's territory where we had the time the night before. He told my uncle and my brother, Crawford, that those chiefs, whom Joel and I had taken, were bad men, and if we had brought them with us, they would have fixed them for us and that those bad chiefs had no more idea of our men going out and jumping onto them, than nothing in the world, and that that was all that saved us. He also stated that the bad Indians did not care how many of their men they lost, just so they accomplished the killing of the white people and got their stock.

Joel kept his word in reference to the wine. He drove the ox team and wagon in which was the wine, also the bedding for uncle's family. He would claim he was sleepy, get the girls to drive for him, get the drinking cup, fill it two-thirds full when their backs were turned, and then come running and holloing for me to hold up, for he wanted a drink, as I had a keg of water in the hind end of my wagon. He would never spill a bit of it. I would drink part of it and Joel never let the rest go to waste. Joel was the prettiest runner I ever saw. He could run so level, that his head looked like it was sailing through the air. I never saw him outrun, and I had seen him run with some who were counted fast. He brought me wine several times. I asked him one day, how much wine there was in that keg.

"O! There's right smart of it," he replied.

I told him not to bring me any more, and that was the last he brought me, but I heard it was dry before we got through.

CHAPTER IV

OVER THE MOUNTAINS INTO CALIFORNIA

While we were going down the Humbolt River, several days before we got to the sink or desert, six of our men got tired going so slow, and went on and left us. Uncle tried to get them to stay with us, but when they would go, he offered them provisions to take along. Four of them were so gritty that they would not take any. Two of them did. These four thought they would come to what were called "trading posts," but they had all gone back to California, as we afterwards found. The men had nearly starved to death. They had to shoot birds and they used everything they could find for food.

These "trading posts" were kept by men who had brought on pack mules, provisions from California, to sell to emigrants and bought up weak stock and herded them on the grass until they got strong enough to drive across the Sierra Nevada Mountains into California.

Uncle thought we would soon come to one of these trading posts, where we could get flour, but the traders had all gone back and ceased to trade. We ran out of flour and sea biscuits when we crossed the desert into Carson Valley. We had to live on beef and mutton for five or six hundred miles. The first flour and bread we got to eat, was after we crossed the summit of the Sierra Nevada Mountains.

I thought I had seen mountains before, but these beat them all. When we got to the headwaters of the Carson River, for it was up in the Sierra Nevada Mountains, we went over what was called the Johnson Cut Off. When we got to the foot of the mountain, I looked up its side and told Uncle Joshua that we could never get up this mountain in this world, for it looked as straight up as a wall could possibly be.

"O, yes, we can," he said. "We will get on the trail and go first one way and then another, until we get up."

We were six days getting everything to the top of that mountain, and when we got up, we rested one night. The first horse uncle lost was getting up this mountain. He was a little weak, stumbled and fell off the trail and that was the last we ever saw of him.

The next morning we yoked up the oxen and all got ready to start. Uncle instructed me to lead out. Right on top of the mountain, it was pretty level for some distance. I drove on ahead of the rest. I came to where I saw I had to go down again. I stopped, locked both hind wheels of my wagon, rough locked them by wrapping a chain twice around the felloe and tire, so the tire would ride on the chain and make it drag hard on the ground. I started down. I had not gone far until I found I was going down the same kind of a mountain we had been six days coming up. A little further down, the trail got very narrow. I was on the left side of the oxen, for that was the side upon which we had always taken when driving. That put me on the lower side, so that if I had been knocked off, that would have been the last of me. I stopped and let the wagon pass me, so that I could get on the upper side to drive. When I crossed behind the wagon, the dust blew up in my face so thick that I could not see my wagon, and that was the last I saw of those oxen until nearly sun down.

I went down the mountain as fast as I could. I had no idea I would ever see those oxen again, but when I got down on level ground at the foot of the mountain, where I could see, off about one hundred yards, there stood my oxen and wagon, right side up. There were three yoke of them, six head of cattle, but my near ox, next to the wheel, died that night.

The first ones to come down following me, were uncle and aunt. They were in a light one-seated top buggy, the one they had used all the way across the plains. Uncle had his feet under the buggy, holding down the hind axle tree, while aunt had the lines, driving. They drove a brown mare, which I had taken from Indiana and a black horse they had fetched from Wisconsin.

Aunt was saying, "O, Bailey, I will be killed, I will be killed."

"Hold on Susan, hold on, Susan," answered uncle.

The team was nearly setting down on their hind parts and just sliding. They could not move their feet to step for rods at a time.

"How did you ever get down that mountain," uncle asked when he saw me.

"I will never tell, uncle," I said.

Nor did I tell, for I could not tell myself how those oxen got down that mountain.

When we got started again on the trail, we met a man going across the mountains, over the same route, with a pack train. He was packing provisions across to the miners in Carson Valley. Uncle coaxed him out of two fifty pound sacks of flour at thirty dollars a sack. This made our first bread since crossing the desert.

Somebody stole the black horse which uncle and aunt drove down the mountain, while we were camped there that night. This was the second horse uncle lost on the trip, and the last one since starting from the states.

We drove down the west slope toward the gold mine. The second night after we left the summit, it commenced to snow on us, but not very fast. Every day after that, it was snowing or raining until we came to the gold mines. Some mornings the snow would be two or three inches deep, but by night we would get to where it was raining.

One night we camped in what was called Pleasant Valley, near a stream called Boland's Run. A man by the name of Thomas Boland, kept a trading post here, with a stock of groceries, clothing, boots and shoes, and a saloon in connection. A little further down, we helped uncle across the McCosma River, to a place called Fair Play, where uncle said that he and his family could get down to their future home alone. We then bade farewell to uncle and family, and started on a prospecting tour.

This was now the last of November.

After we got to California, we found out that those bad Indians on the Humbolt River, had taken two or three messes or camps, that year, and one man escaped from one of the camps and two out of another, the rest of the men, women and children being killed. These men, who got away from among the Indians in some way or other, got to other camps. The trains that were taken, were camped no great distance apart; far enough so as to herd their stock and keep them separate. They said the Indians holloed on one side and while the campers were looking in the direction of the holloing, the first thing they knew, other Indians came right in on them behind their backs.

These three remaining men said that the next morning they gathered the white men from the camps up and down the river, and followed on the trail of the marauders. The Indians had cut open sacks of flour and scattered it along their trail. They had also cut open feather beds and the feathers were blown over the prairie. When the white men came in sight, the Indians broke and ran in every direction, and when they got up to the captured oxen and wagons, which the Indians had taken from the campers, it was found that the Indians had cooked and were eating an unyoked ox, with the other ox still yoked with the dead one. They did not know how to get the yoke off. The men took what oxen and stock they could find, along with them, but had no time to stay to hunt for them. This is the story of the men who escaped, and were then living in California.

These campers must have driven until after dark, for it seemed they did not have their oxen unyoked, for we always unyoked our oxen as soon as we stopped.

I shall now try to give you a description of the country through which we traveled. Starting in Nebraska, there was what I considered pretty good land for two or three hundred miles, though I did not see very much of the country outside the Platte River bottom. After we came to the Rocky Mountains, I never saw very much of what I called good land laying in one body. Sometimes we would come to some pretty fair rolling land, but it was what I called poor and rough. At times we got so high up, we were above timber line, but we always had grass where there was soil. We passed through sage brush and sand, and all of that kind of country looked desolate to me, but once in awhile, we would come to prairie land. We found some pretty good, rich strips of land away out on the other side of the Rocky Mountains. A good long ways out, we came to such a strip of land, which was called Fur Grove, covered with what we called balsam fir.

I do not know in what state it is now, for the whole country from the Missouri River to California was then known as Indian Territory.

Sometimes we would be on the mountain tops, where we could look down and see below where we saw a fog, or at least thought so, but the men said it was raining down in the valley, but clear where we were.

We passed near Red Mountains and there were black mountains not very far apart and which could be seen from one point of view. We crossed some small rivers. I remember one in particular we had to cross on one of those willow brush bridges. There had been so much travel on this bridge, that a great hole was worn in it, but uncle said we did not have time to stop to mend it, and we would have to risk it. We got the horses, sheep, oxen and wagons across on the bridge, but the cattle we had to swim the river. I don't believe I ever heard what the name of that river was, if I did, I have forgotten it.

I did not see much of Iowa on this trip. Of all the country I saw from Indiana, through, or after I got through, there was none suited me like Central Illinois, and I have not changed my mind. There was government land in Illinois to enter at that time.

CHAPTER V

PROSPECTING FOR GOLD – SOME HARD EXPERIENCES

After we left uncle in the mining district called Fair Play, we crossed back over the McCosma River to Boland's Run and went over to Four Spring Valley and prospected for some time before we struck any gold that paid. We finally struck a claim that paid six dollars a day to the hand, clear of water. We had to buy water from a dike that was dug around on the side of the mountain and which cost us four dollars a day. We worked on this claim about three weeks, when the dike broke between where we were at work and the head of the dike where the dam was made across the McCosma River to turn the water out into the dike. We could not work any more until the dike was mended.

My brother, Crawford Bailey and Wint Crumly went out prospecting. They went back across the McCosma River into Fair Play district, where we had parted with Uncle Joshua, a distance of fourteen miles. They struck a surface digging, and they wrote me and I went to them. We had to buy water at the same price, one dollar an inch, or four dollars a day. This claim was richer of gold. We made nine dollars a day to the hand, clear of water.

We finally heard that the dike was mended over at Four Springs Valley and I went over and sold our provisions and collected sixty dollars we had loaned to a miner by the name of Thomas Brison. We did not go back to Four Springs Valley to work any more, but remained on the claim at Fair Play, until in June, when the water gave out and we could not get water to wash any longer. We then concluded to go north on to the American, Uby and Feather rivers and prospect and see if we could strike claims where we could get water to wash with.

The American River was the next river after leaving the McCosma. When we came to the American River, up in the gold region, where we were crossing, the mountains were very steep and looked like they were straight up. We had to travel six miles to get from the bottom of the mountain to its top. But when we got to the American River district, every place we went, we found it claimed up and plenty of miners at work to do all the work there was to do. We could neither find claims to work for ourselves, nor could we hire out to work for any one else.

We left the American River and went over the mountains to the Uby River. When we got on top of the mountains and started down toward Uby River, we had a hard time finding the path. There was so much gravel and rock and so little soil or dirt, it was almost impossible to see where footmen had made the path. Far toward the west end of the mountain, pack animals could get on top and then travel east ward from where we were crossing, but nothing except footmen and Indians could cross on the trail we were using.

Woodmen had packed their wagons and tools up this mountain somewhere to the westward, to the point where we were crossing, and had cut sawlogs and hauled or rolled them nearby. Then by rolling the logs three or four rods on sloping ground, they would fall straight down to the river bottom, a distance that took us fellows a half day to go up.

I was hunting for the trail which led down the mountain, when I came to the sloping ground where the woodmen had rolled these logs off. I walked carefully down this place, and when I looked down, I saw a yellow streak straight below me. It looked like I could step across it, but I knew it was a river. It made me dizzy to look over the precipice and I stepped backward a few paces and then turned to walk to the top of the mountain again. If I had slipped there, that would have been the last of me.

After hunting a good while, we found the trail and went down the mountain. The path was just wide enough for one to walk on. If a person had stepped off with one foot, the rest of his life's story would have certainly been very brief. When we got down to the river, that little yellow streak which I thought I could step across when looking down the mountain, we had to cross in a ferry boat, the Uby River being a quarter of a mile wide.

We went north and northeast until we reached Morisson's Diggings. The snow at this place was over thirty feet deep in the winter. They had to lay in provisions in the fall to last them all winter and until the snow melted off, and the mountain dried so the ground on the side of the mountains got solid enough so that the trail would not slip off from under the feet of the pack mules.

They built their houses out of round pine or fur logs, a foot and a half in diameter, and porches built by letting one log at the eaves of the house run out and logs a foot through, for posts set up under the ends of these logs. These porches were used to put wood under for winter use. When the snow commenced falling, they would beat it back with their shovels and keep it beaten back until they could form an arch overhead, making a tunnel from one house to another, so they could visit each other during the winter.

It was the twentieth day of July when we got there and they were just getting started to wash gold. The gold was mixed with dirt and quartz rock. These rocks were round and smooth and about the size of a man's fist. When they were washed in the sluice boxes and thrown in piles, they looked as white as snow. I have often thought what a beautiful walk or drive they would make if we had them in Illinois.

We stopped at Morisson's Diggings two or three days. We found Uncle Isaac and his son, Jesse, at this place. We left there and went across another mountain to a place called Poker Flat, which was fourteen miles over the mountain. We heard there, that across on the other side of another mountain, on a stream called Nelson Creek, were new diggings. Uncle Isaac and his son made us promise, that if we heard of new diggings being struck, to give them word. I went back the next day and told them and they returned with me over to Poker Flat, where brother Crawford and the four others were waiting for us.

We went over the mountain to Nelson Creek. An old Scotchman by the name of Wright, had struck a rich claim on the side of the creek on a little bottom. The gold here was coarser than it was in the southern diggings. The gold that Mr. Wright was getting, looked like small potatoes. Some were a little less and some a little over one ounce in weight. We prospected all around there, but could not strike any pay dirt. We concluded that if there was gold on this bottom, there must be gold in the creek. We put six men to dig a ditch to turn the creek out of the channel and then dam the creek and turn the water out, so we could get to the bottom of the creek.

Old Mr. Wright had packed a whip saw over to make lumber for sluice boxes. Uncle Isaac and I borrowed the saw and went to work and whipsawed lumber for sluice boxes. We cut down two trees, up as high as we could reach, then cut small trees for skids, laid one end of the skid on the side of the mountain and the other end of the skids on the stumps of the trees we cut off, then rolled the log up on these skids. Then with pick and shovel, a level place was dug underneath, the length of the sawlog, barked and lined it on two sides, then sawed to the lines. One stood on top of the log, the other under it, or in the pit, as it was called. The whipsaw is shaped like one of the common key saws, wide at one end and narrow at the other, only the whipsaw had handles on both ends. It took nice work to whipsaw lumber and keep it true to the line.

We got our lumber sawed, our sluice boxes made, our ditch dug, our creek damed and the creek turned out of the channel, prepared to work in the bed of the creek.

Late one evening, we just had time to roll over a large bolder and get a pan of sand and gravel, and pan it out. We dried the gold and weighed it and there was seventy-five dollars worth of gold in that one pan. We worked out this claim, but it proved to be a slate rock bed and was smooth and sleek, and the water washed all the gold away, only where a huge bolder was imbeded in the slate bed and the gold settled around the bolders. We did not get any more gold out of the rest of that claim, than I got in that one pan.

We left Uncle Isaac at this claim and followed down Nelson Creek. Our party was composed of Crawford Bailey, Winston Crumly, Jack Alberts, Guss Parberry, Bird Farris and myself. There was a nice path beat down on the side of the creek, but the mountains on both sides stood almost straight up. We went down the creek, fifteen or twenty miles, when we suddenly came to a waterfall where the water dropped straight down about forty or fifty rods. There was no way for us to get down. We then thought the people who made the path, had to climb the mountains. We looked up on our right hand and could see the dirt crumbling out from between the rocks. It was straight up. We saw there was no show to go up on that side. We looked up on our left and could not see any dirt or rock crumbling off this mountain.

We concluded that they must have climbed up over this mountain to get out. We started up. We could hardly keep from falling backwards. We held to little vines or little fine brush which grew out from between the layers of rock. Finally, after we had gone up a distance of perhaps a couple of miles, we could see above us a shelf of rock extending out over our heads. It then dawned upon us that the path we had followed down the creek, had been made by people who had come that far and were compelled to go back and that no one had ever gone up this mountain.

We looked as far as we could see each way, but that shelf of rock stood out over our heads from three to six or eight feet. We were sure that when we got up to that shelf, we could not get over it, neither could we go back down again; for one can go up when one can see where to stick their toes, but cannot see to go down without falling. We began to think we were where we could not get away alive. We looked off to our left and saw one place in this shelf that was narrower than the rest, and we concluded to make for that place with the possibility that we might be able to break off some of the rock and get above. It was still a good ways up from where we were. We made for the narrow shelf, but when we got there, the rock was so hard that we could not pierce it with our picks, but the mountain was not quite so steep under this piece of shelf. My brother said to me:

"If you will pick in the side of the mountain and stick your toes in so you will have a good foothold, and hold against my back with my shovel, and two of the other men, one on each side of me, fix their feet so they can lift me on their picks while I hold to the shelf, I will try and see how it looks above."

Two of our strongest men lifted him on their picks while I held against his back with the shovel until he was high enough to look above the shelf.

"The mountain," he said, "is not steep above here, and it is not far to the top, if we could only get over this shelf. Let me put one foot on one pick and the other foot on the other pick and you fellows lift me up as high as you can. Wash, you hold against my back and if I can get a little farther up, I can catch some brush and pull myself up over the shelf." They lifted and I held him to the shelf, while he climbed up over it. We reached him a shovel and a pick. He dug a good place in which to set his feet, and then reached the shovel over the bench, for one of the boys to catch hold. We lifted one of the boys, while Crawford pulled him up. We kept this process up until all were up but one. We left the lightest one to the last. He was down where he couldn't see any of us and he got scared and trembled and claimed that he did not believe he could hold to the shovel for us to draw him up. We dug holes to set our heels in and then held others by the feet so they could look down over the shelf and see and talk to him. He was pale and greatly frightened. I got some of the men to hold me by the feet while I encouraged him. I told him to take a good hold of the shovel and as soon as he came to where I was and got him by the arm, he could count himself safe. I don't believe that there ever was a white man or an Indian, who ever went up that mountain before, nor since the last man we got up.

About two miles from where we got on the top of the mountain, we came to a mining town, called Poor Man's Diggings. We could not get work there. We prospected for a few days, but could find no gold, although there were a good many good, paying claims belonging to other men. We left there and went to what was called American Valley, where a man struck a rich claim. This was called a rich claim, because it would pay one hundred dollars or over to the hand a day. We tried to hire out and work by the day, but they had all the hands they could work. Everywhere up north, they paid a man at least five dollars a day.

We left the American Valley country, which was on the headwaters of the Feather River, and struck for the Sacramento River Valley. We thought we might find work on a ranch.

We went down to Marysville. The Uba River enters the Sacramento below Marysville and the Feather River above. Farming was all done when we got down there, so we could not find work. We then struck for Sacramento City. As a fellow would say, we were getting "about strapped," that is, running short of money. We walked from Marysville to the American River bridge one night, about fifty miles. We ate breakfast there, walked twenty miles up the American River and about three o'clock that day, hired to work for the next morning at two dollars and seventy-five cents per day, and board ourselves. I worked for a man by the name of Stewart. I was to work two weeks, but I worked ten days.

We went from here back to Fair Play, from where we had started. We stayed there until November. The weather kept dry—had no rain, so Uncle Joshua came to us and wanted us to work for him on a ranch in the Sacramento Valley, above the city of Sacramento something like three hundred miles, between the towns of Tehama and Red Bluffs. We worked for him ten months at fifty dollars a month.

My brother got sick and went to the mountains and I worked one month for a man by the name of David Jorden and his partner, Joseph Moran, in a brick yard, for fifty dollars. When uncle paid us, and I received my pay for working at the brick yard, I went to my brother, sixty miles southeast of Sacramento, to a mining town called Volcano.

We remained in Volcano for about two weeks. We then went to Sacramento. From there we took a steamboat to San Francisco, where we stayed for two weeks. We then got on a steamship and sailed for Panama. We landed once at a town in Mexico, called Acapuco, to take on beef cattle. We were fourteen days on the way from San Francisco to Panama. We remained in Panama one night, and then took a train and crossed the isthmus by railroad, which was the first railroad train I ever saw.

The next day we arrived at Aspinwall, now called Colon, where we stayed until the next day, when we boarded a ship bound for New York. We were nine days on the way from Aspinwall, or Colon, to New York City. We then took a steamboat and went up the Hudson River to Albany, where we took a train to Buffalo; from there to Cleveland, Ohio; to Indianapolis, and then to LaFayette, Ind. I then went to my home in Fountain County, and later came to Cheney's Grove, Illinois, on horse back. I landed at Cheney's Grove on New Year's Day, 1856.